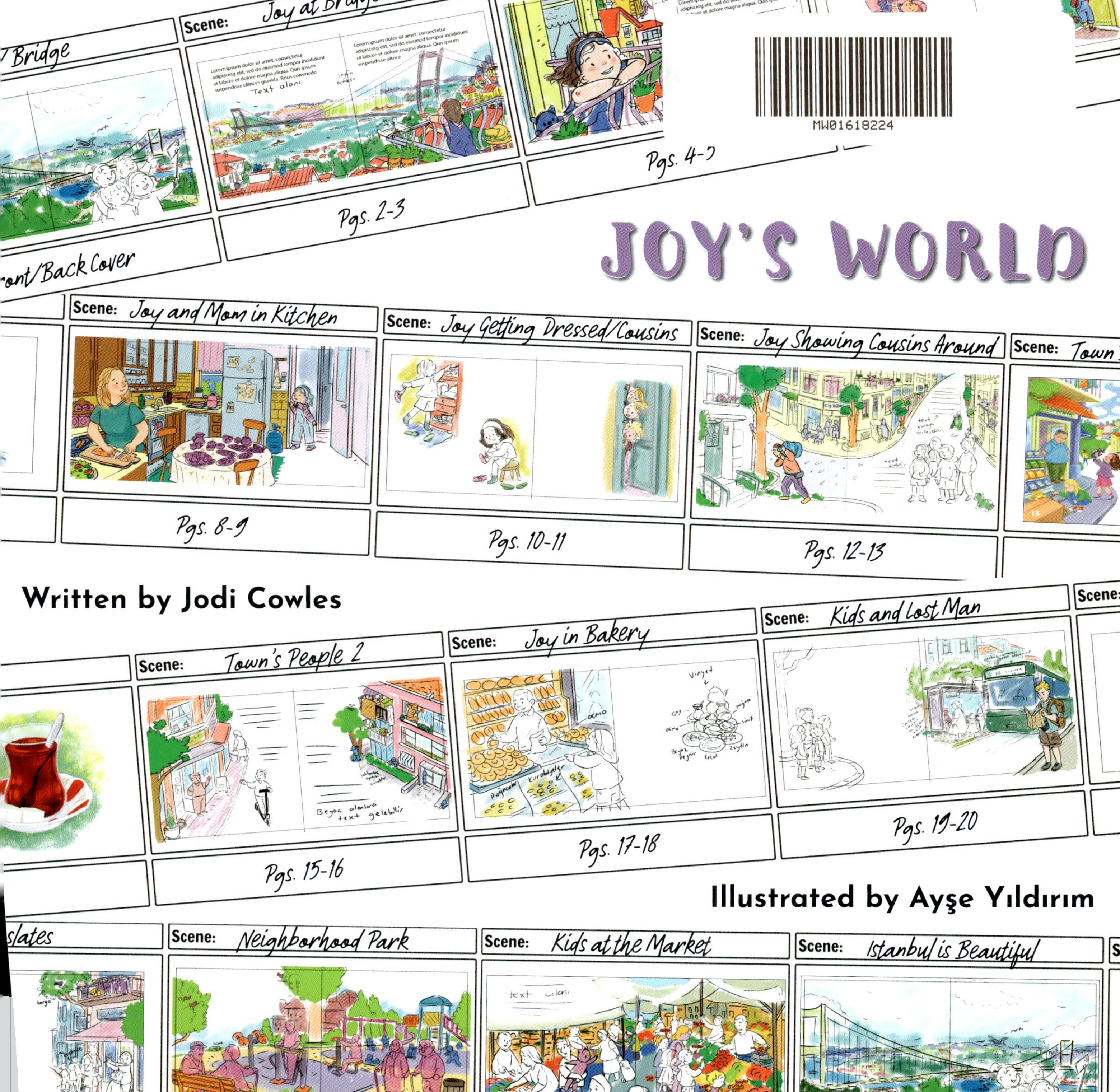

JOY'S WORLD
Written by Jodi Cowles
Illustrated by Ayşe Yıldırım
Bridge
Front/Back Cover
Scene: Joy at Bridge
Lorem ipsum dolor sit amet, consectetur adipiscing elit, sed do eiusmod tempor incididunt ut labore et dolore magna aliqua. Quis ipsum suspendisse ultrices gravida. Risus commodo
Text alanı
Lorem ipsum dolor sit amet, consectetur adipiscing elit, sed do eiusmod tempor incididunt ut labore et dolore magna aliqua. Quis ipsum suspendisse ultrices
Pgs. 2-3
Text
Lorem ipsum dolor sit amet, consectetur adipiscing elit, sed do eiusmod tempor incididunt ut labore et dolore magna aliqua. Quis ipsum
Pgs. 4-7
MW01618224
Scene: Joy and Mom in Kitchen
Pgs. 8-9
Scene: Joy Getting Dressed/Cousins
Pgs. 10-11
Scene: Joy Showing Cousins Around
Pgs. 12-13
Scene: Town's
Scene: Town's People 2
Beyaz alanlara text gelebilir
Pgs. 15-16
Scene: Joy in Bakery
Pgs. 17-18
Scene: Kids and Lost Man
Pgs. 19-20
Scene:
slates
Scene: Neighborhood Park
Scene: Kids at the Market
text alanı
Scene: Istanbul is Beautiful

For my Joy, to help you remember.

Joy'cum, hatırlamana yardımcı olmak için.

Welcome to Türkiye!

To request permissions, contact the author, or order books in other language combinations, visit joysworldbooks.com.

Softcover ISBN: 978-1-961736-03-0
Hardcover ISBN: 978-1-961736-05-4
Ebook ISBN: 978-1-961736-04-7

First edition 2024

Written by: Jodi Cowles
Illustrated by: Ayşe Yıldırım
Layout by: Paige Elliott

Printed in China

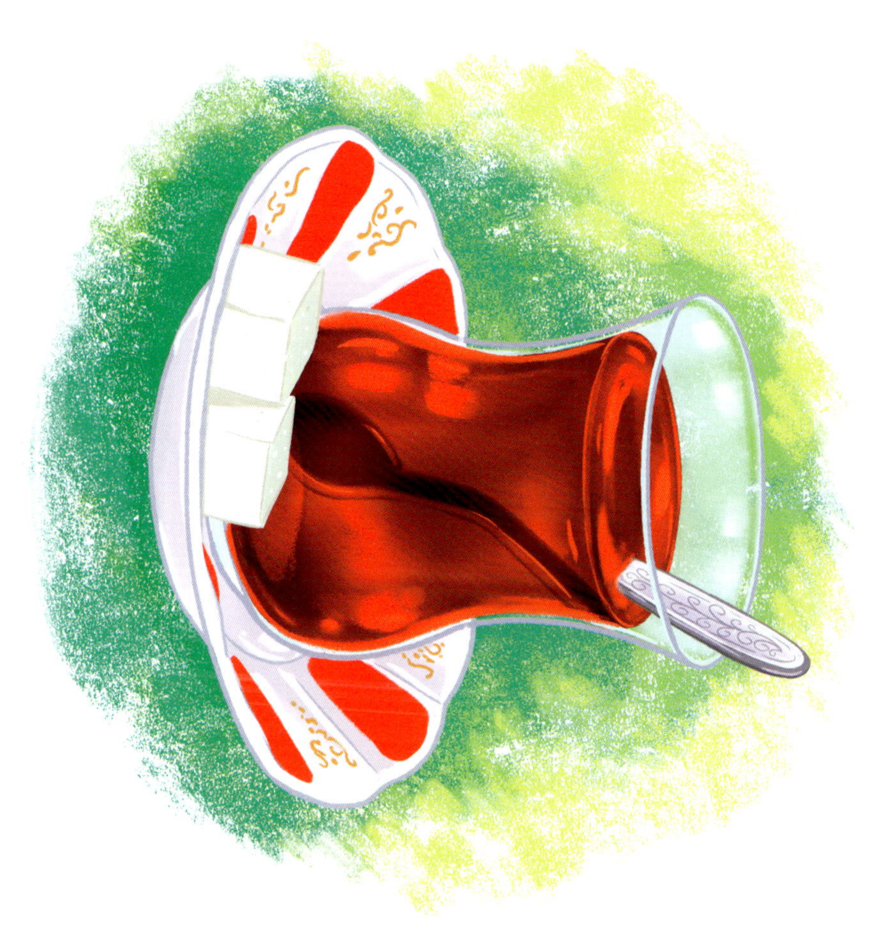

Merhaba! Benim adım Joy!

Oh, sorry! I should have asked if you speak Turkish first. I said, "Hello, my name is Joy!"

This is me and my cat, Beauty! Right now we're looking out at the Bosphorous. Well, I'm looking. Beauty is having a nap because yorgunluktan öldü.

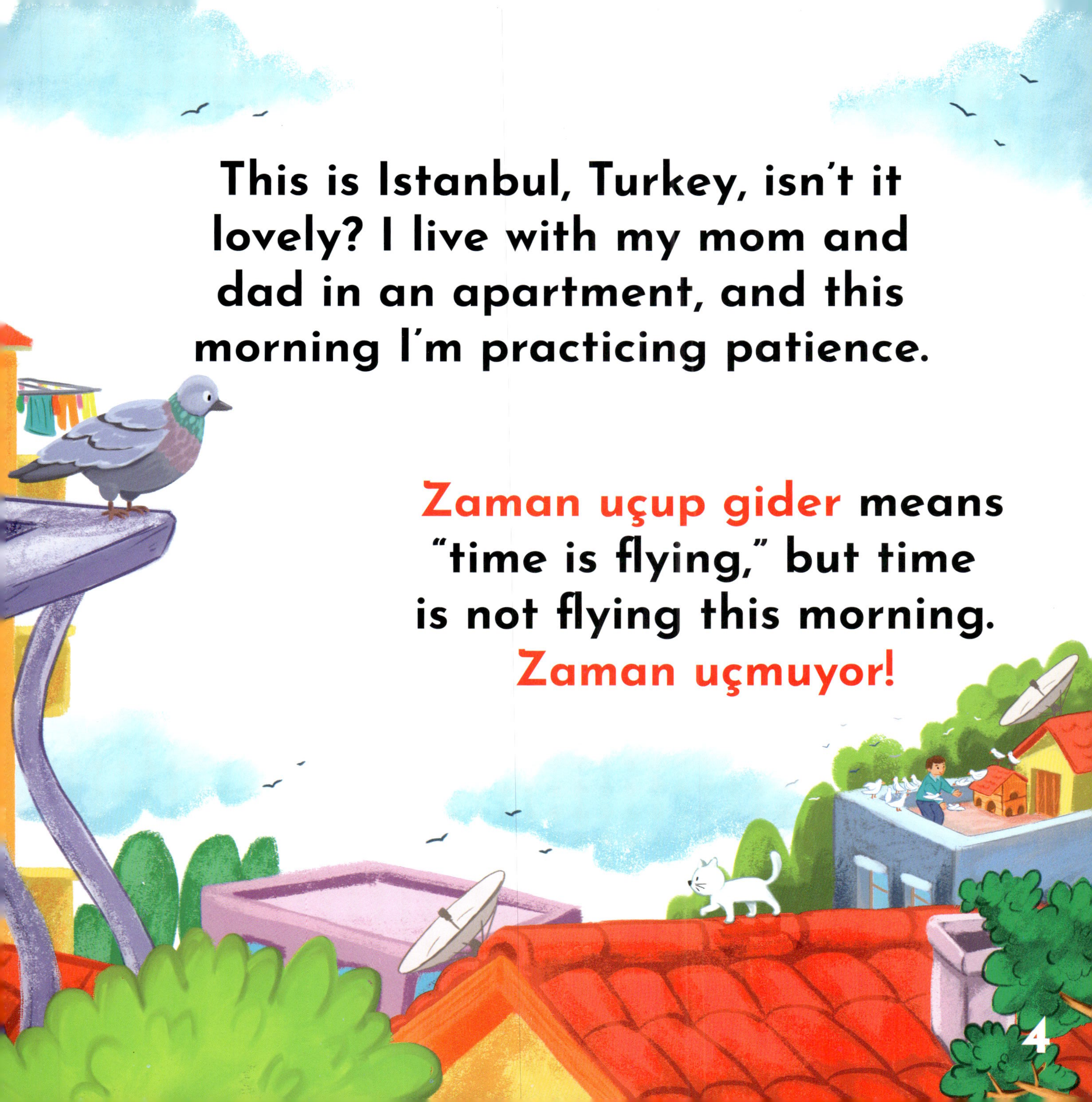

This is Istanbul, Turkey, isn't it lovely? I live with my mom and dad in an apartment, and this morning I'm practicing patience.

Zaman uçup gider means "time is flying," but time is not flying this morning. Zaman uçmuyor!

You see, my cousins from America arrived last night after I was already in bed.

And they're still not awake!

So far this morning
I have read all my
favorite books,

colored five
pictures,

and waited
sessiz sessiz
at their door.

"Anne, are they ever going to wake up?" But Mom is used to me being impatient. "Sabırlı ol!" she says. "Why don't you go to the bakkal for me? Peynir, domates ve simit almam lazım."

In Turkey no one wears **ayakkabılar** inside the house, so I take off my slippers and grab my favorite shoes.

Mor means purple, but if you want to say "more" you say **çok** which is pronounced "choke," but not like "I'll choke you!" Languages can be confusing!

Before I head
out the door
I hear voices
calling out,
"Wait for us!
Wait for us!"

Sonunda!
My cousins
are finally
awake!

It doesn't take
them long to
get dressed,
and we head
out the door.

I can't wait
to show my
cousins around
my
neighborhood!

Would you like to join us?

BAKKAL
MANAV

This is the bakkal. It's only one minute up the road and I love coming here. Dede and Teyze own the bakkal and I love them even more than the abur cubur they give me or the hulahop we play together!

I teach my cousins how to say günaydın, which means "good morning." Can you say it, too?

"goo-NIE-dun!"

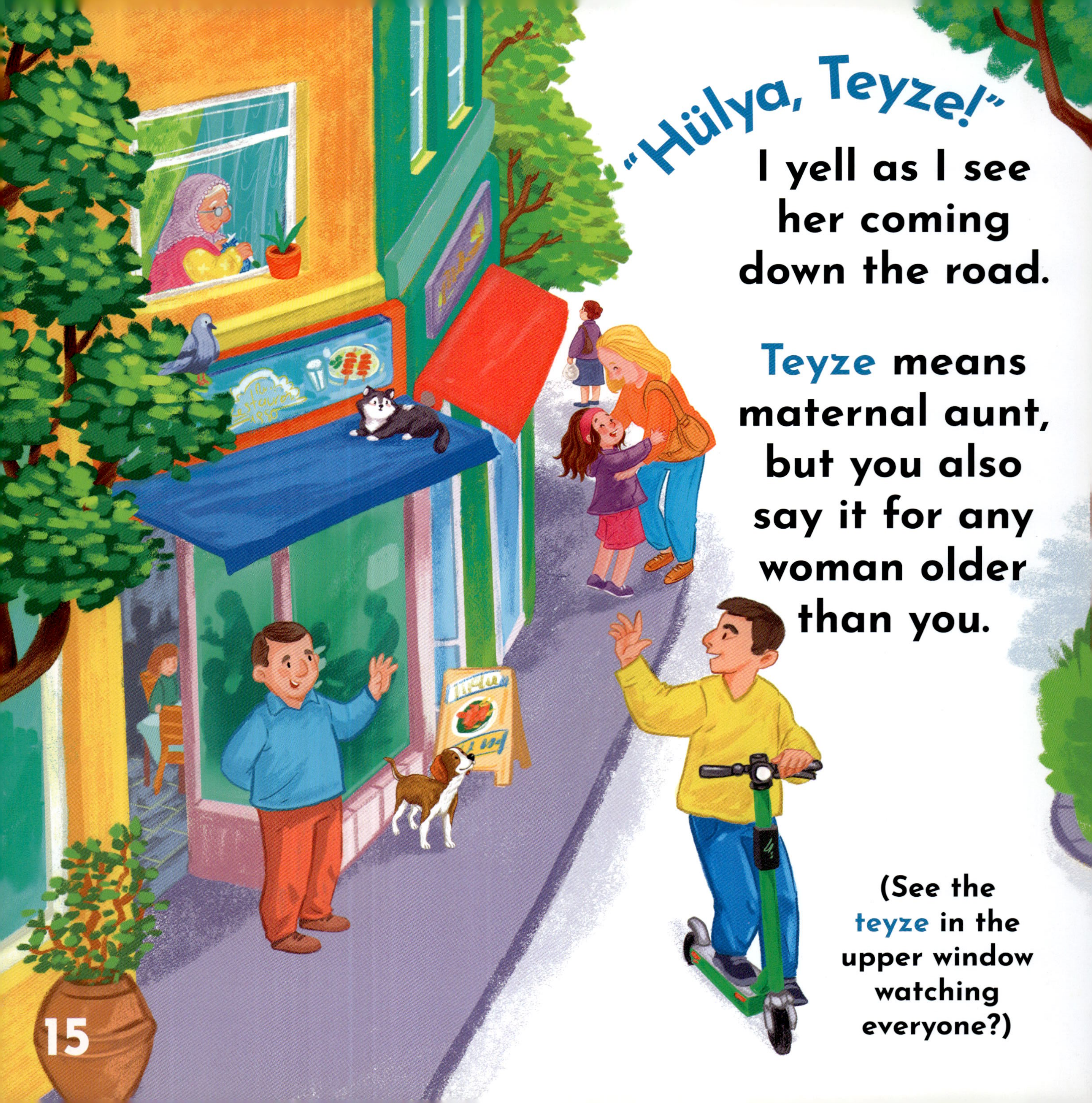

"Hülya, Teyze!" I yell as I see her coming down the road.

Teyze means maternal aunt, but you also say it for any woman older than you.

(See the teyze in the upper window watching everyone?)

They're playing saklambaç!

This is the fırın, and mis gibi kokuyor.

"Altı simit, dört açma, ve on iki kurabiye lütfen."

The fırıncı knows my mom didn't really ask for cookies, but he winks anyway and says, "Afiyet olsun."

I teach my cousins how to say thank you, but you should probably learn it, too. "Teşekkür ederim." It's kind of like "te-shek-coor eh-dare-im."

That's the bus that takes me to Turkish school! I love my Turkish school, especially dans dans and piyano.

Does this man look lost to you?

43R
RUMELİ HİSARÜSTÜ

He IS lost! And he's German!

"I am lost," he says. "Do you know Hagia Sophia where is?"

The abi tells me where to go. I tell the German, and he says, "Danke!"

I love

translating

for people!

This is our neighborhood park. I love coming here to meet my friend Mahinur. (That's her on the scooter.)

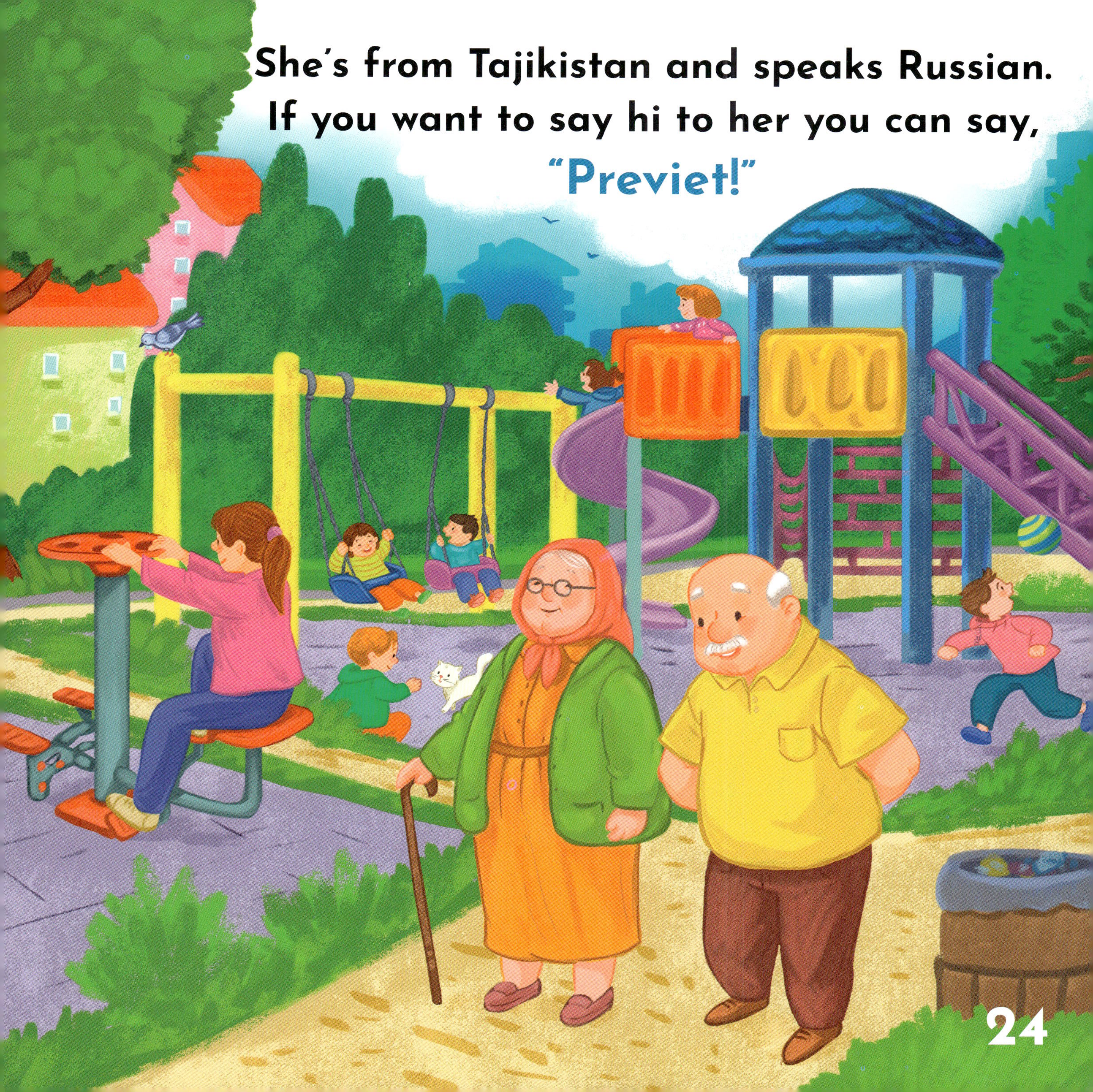

She’s from Tajikistan and speaks Russian.
If you want to say hi to her you can say,
“Previet!”

Just tomatoes and cheese today,
but maybe you can see why we
love coming to the pazar.
Yummy things everywhere!

Isn't Istanbul beautiful?
You can say it's çok güzel!

I hope you'll come visit sometime like my cousins have. Until then, **görüşürüz!**

Glossary

Merhaba (1)	Hello
Benim adım... (1)	My name is...
yorgunluktan öldü (2)	She is dead tired
Zaman uçup gider (4)	Time is flying
Zaman uçmuyor (4)	Time is not flying
sessiz sessiz (6)	quiet quiet
anne (8)	mom
sabırlı ol (8)	be patient
bakkal (8, 14)	small store
peynir (8)	cheese

Glossary

domates (8)	tomatoes
ve (8, 18)	and
simit (8, 18)	bagel
almam lazım (8)	I need to buy
ayakkabılar (9)	shoes
mor (9)	purple
çok (9)	many
sonunda (10)	finally
dede (14)	grandpa
teyze (14, 15)	aunt

Glossary

abur cubur (14)	junk food
hulahop (14)	hula hoop
günaydın (14)	good morning
Hülya (15)	teyze's name, "daydream"
saklambaç (16)	hide and seek
fırın (18)	bakery
bir, iki, üç, dört (18), beş	1, 2, 3, 4, 5
altı (18), yedi, sekiz,	6, 7, 8,
dokuz, on	9, 10
kurabiye (18)	cookie
lütfen (18)	please

Glossary

fırıncı (18)	baker
afiyet olsun (18)	enjoy!
teşekkür ederim (18)	thank you
dans dans (19)	dance
piyano (19)	piano
abi / ağabey (21)	brother
danke (21)	thank you (in German)
previet (24)	hello (in Russian)
pazar (25)	market
çok güzel (27)	very nice
görüşürüz! (28)	see you later!

About Joy's World Bilingual Books for Children

The Joy's World books are inspired by my bilingual, language-loving, third-culture kid, Joy. She was born in Istanbul, Turkey, and didn't set foot in another country until she was almost four years old. According to her, she speaks "all the languages," but if you were to test her, she'd be most fluent in English and Turkish. Although she's just started Spanish immersion preschool, so I'm going to have to start calling her trilingual pretty soon.

This book series is for her, and for all the other bi- and multilingual children like her, growing up around the world, in and out of their passport countries. It's for kids who love languages and cultures, and for the parents who want them to know more about this beautiful world they're growing up in.

Other language combinations

German/Turkish

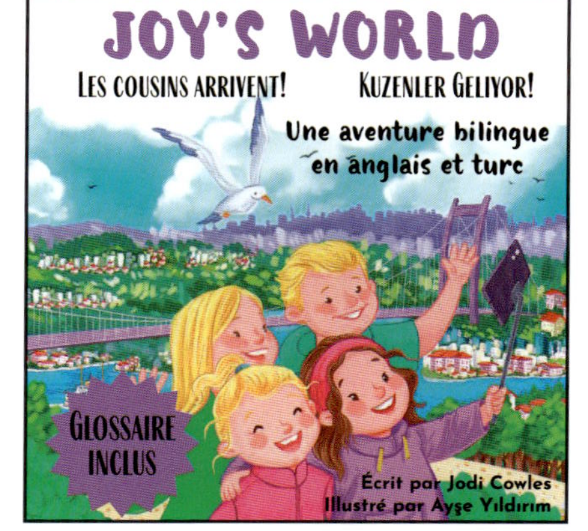

French/Turkish

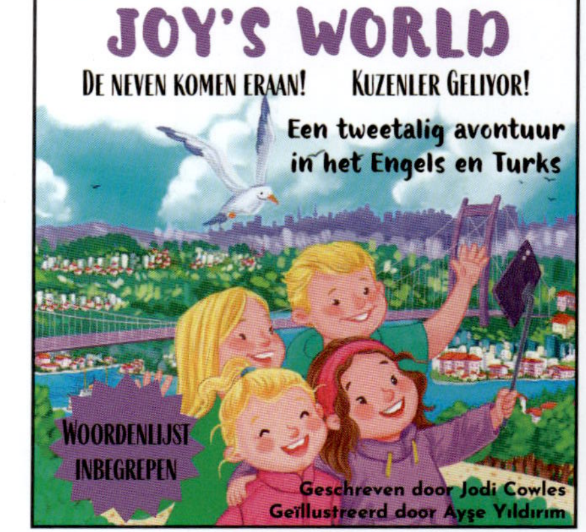

Dutch/Turkish

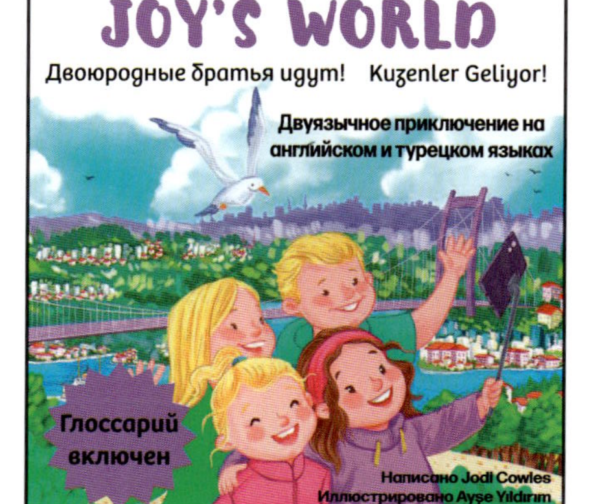

Russian/Turkish

Italian/Turkish

Available at joysworldbooks.com

Danish/Turkish

Bangla/Turkish

Chinese/Turkish

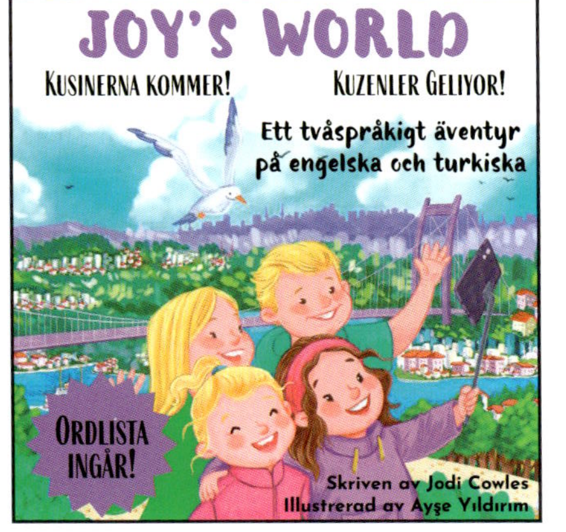

Swedish/Turkish

Spanish/Turkish

Korean/Turkish

I hope you'll visit me again soon!

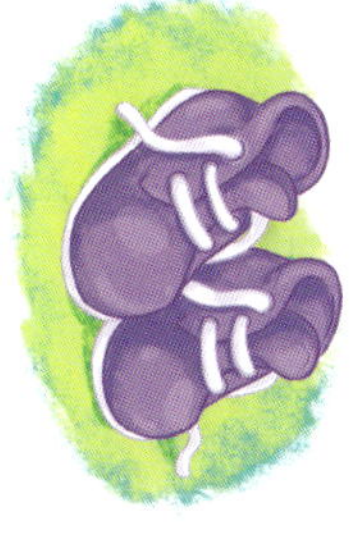
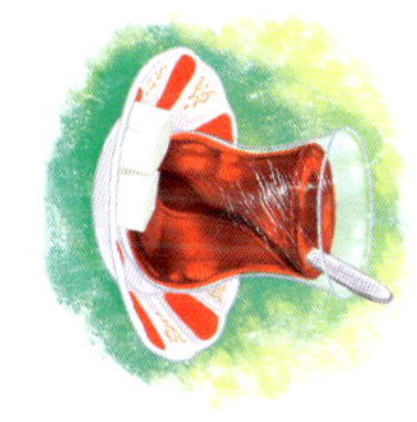

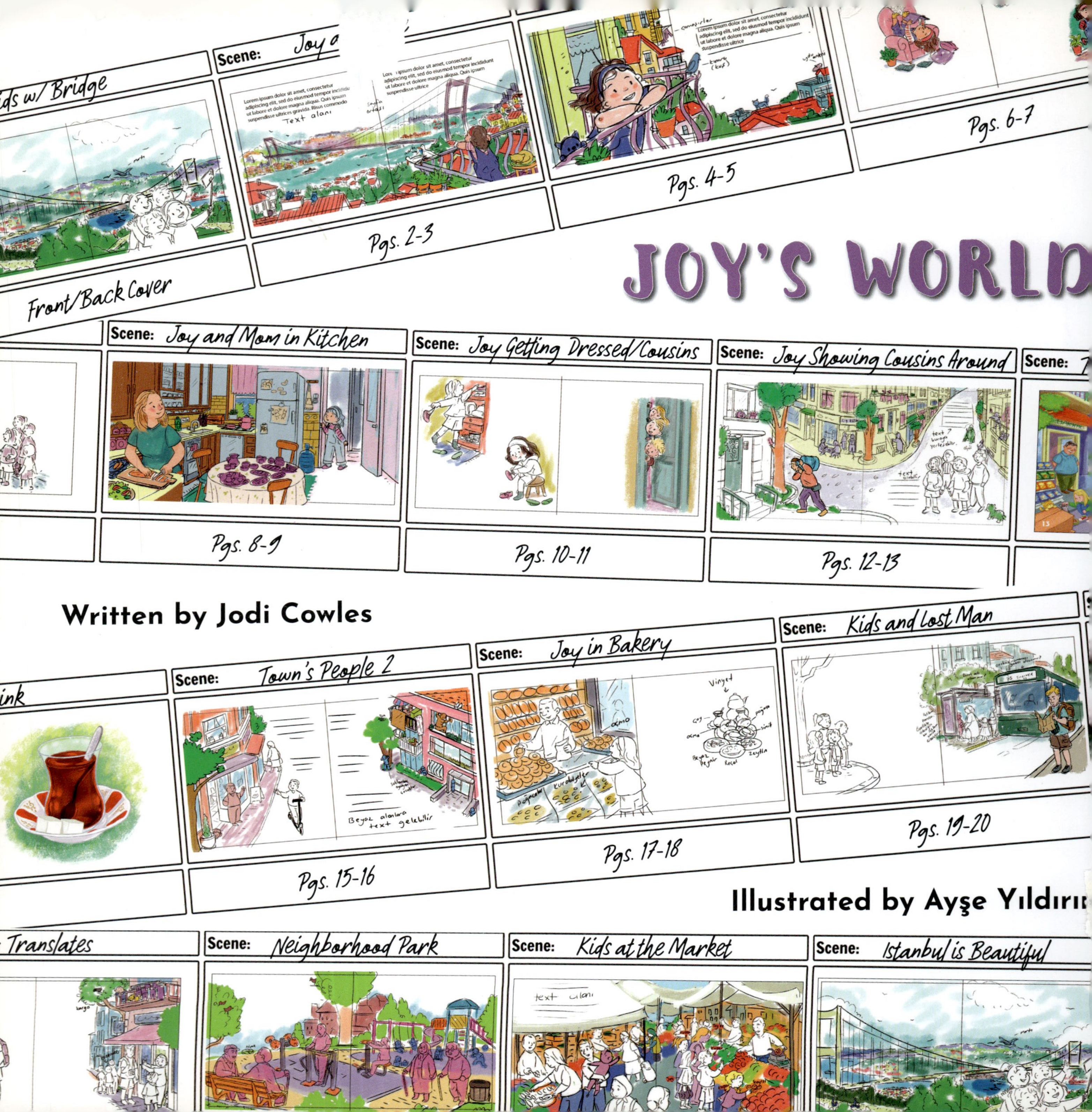

JOY'S WORLD
Written by Jodi Cowles
Illustrated by Ayşe Yıldırı
Scene: Joy a
ids w/ Bridge
Front/Back Cover
Pgs. 2-3
Pgs. 4-5
Pgs. 6-7
Scene: Joy and Mom in Kitchen
Scene: Joy Getting Dressed/Cousins
Scene: Joy Showing Cousins Around
Pgs. 8-9
Pgs. 10-11
Pgs. 12-13
ink
Scene: Town's People 2
Scene: Joy in Bakery
Scene: Kids and Lost Man
Pgs. 15-16
Pgs. 17-18
Pgs. 19-20
Translates
Scene: Neighborhood Park
Scene: Kids at the Market
Scene: Istanbul is Beautiful